Tadpole Books are published by Jump!, 5357 Penn Avenue South, Minneapolis, MN 55419, www.jumplibrary.com

Copyright ©2021 Jump! International copyright reserved in all countries. No part of this book may be reproduced in any form without written permission from the publisher.

Editor: Jenna Gleisner **Designer:** Anna Peterson **Translator:** Annette Granat

Photo Credits: ZSSD/Minden Pictures/SuperStock, cover; Capuski/iStock, 1; ullstein bild/Getty, 2tr, 3; Vadim Petrakov/Shutterstock, 2ml, 4–5; EvergreenPlanet/Shutterstock, 2br, 6–7; Irina Borsuchenko/Dreamstime, 2mr, 2tl, 8–9; Atrium/iStock, 2bl, 10–11; Fernando Calmon/Shutterstock, 12–13; nok6716/iStock, 14–15; Sergio_Mourao/Shutterstock, 16.

Library of Congress Cataloging-in-Publication Data
Names: Nilsen, Genevieve, author.
Title: Los cachorros de los carpinchos / por Genevieve Nilsen. Other titles: Capybara pups. Spanish
Description: Minneapolis, MN: Jump!, Inc., 2021. | Series: Los bebés de la selva | Includes index.
Audience: Grades K–1 | Audience: Ages 3–6
Identifiers: LCCN 2020013154 (print) | LCCN 2020013155 (ebook) | ISBN 9781645276524 (hardcover)
ISBN 9781645276531 (paperback) | ISBN 9781645276548 (ebook)
Subjects: LCSH: Capybara—Infancy—Juvenile literature.
Classification: LCC QL737.R662 N5518 2021 (print) | LCC QL737.R662 (ebook) | DDC 599.35/9—dc23
LC record available at https://lccn.loc.gov/2020013154
LC ebook record available at https://lccn.loc.gov/2020013155

LOS BEBÉS DE LA SELVA

LOS CACHORROS DE LOS CARPINCHOS

por Genevieve Nilsen

TABLA DE CONTENIDO

Palabras a saber..................................2

Los cachorros de los carpinchos..........3

¡Repasemos!....................................16

Índice..16

PALABRAS A SABER

cabeza

cachorros

grupo

orejas

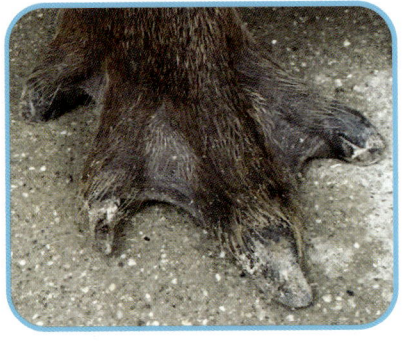
palmeadas

pelo

LOS CACHORROS DE LOS CARPINCHOS

cachorros

¡Estos son cachorros de carpinchos!

Ellos viven en un grupo.

pelo

Tienen el pelo de color café.

Tienen la cabeza grande.

oreja

cabeza

Tienen las orejas pequeñas.

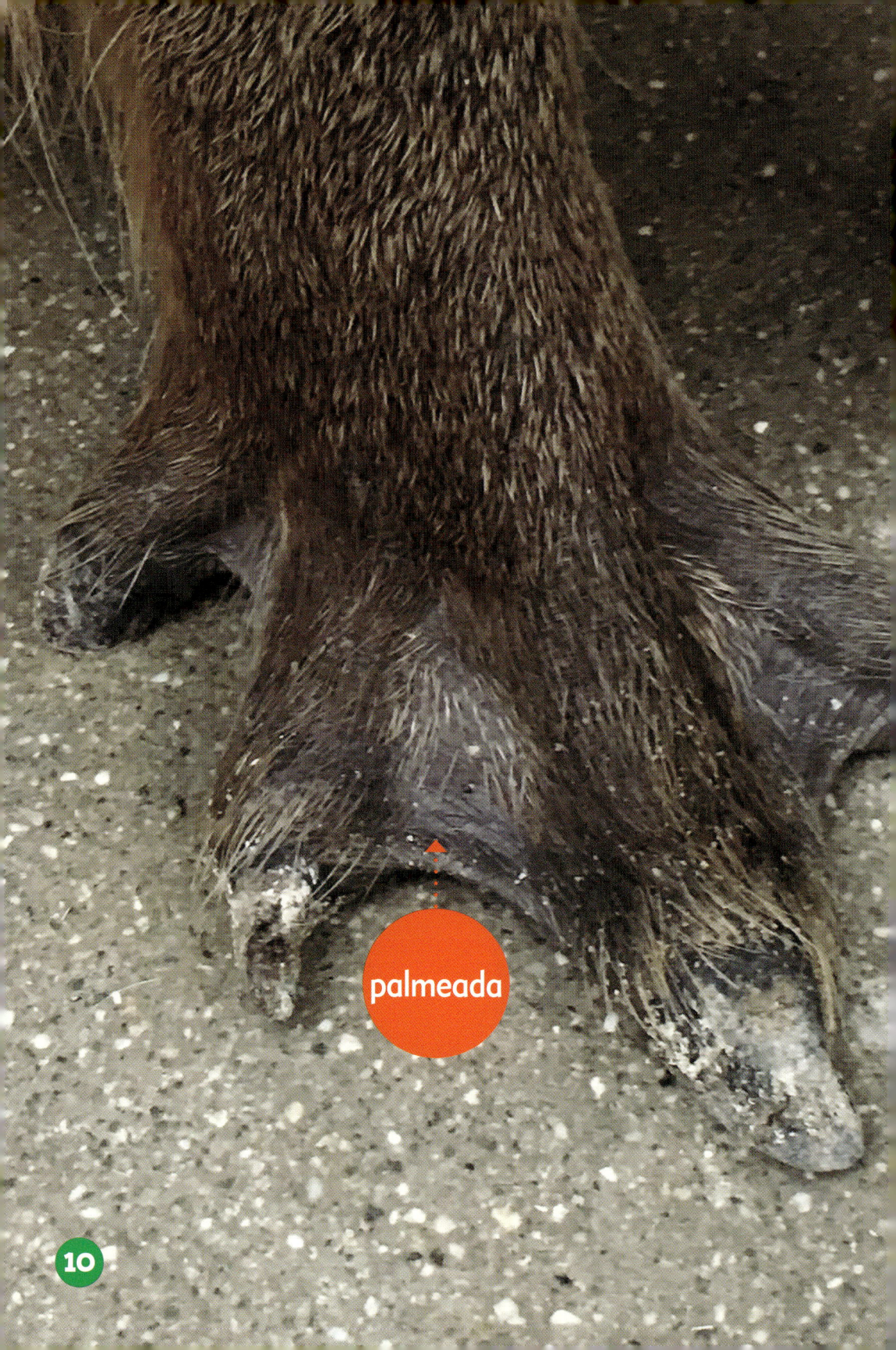

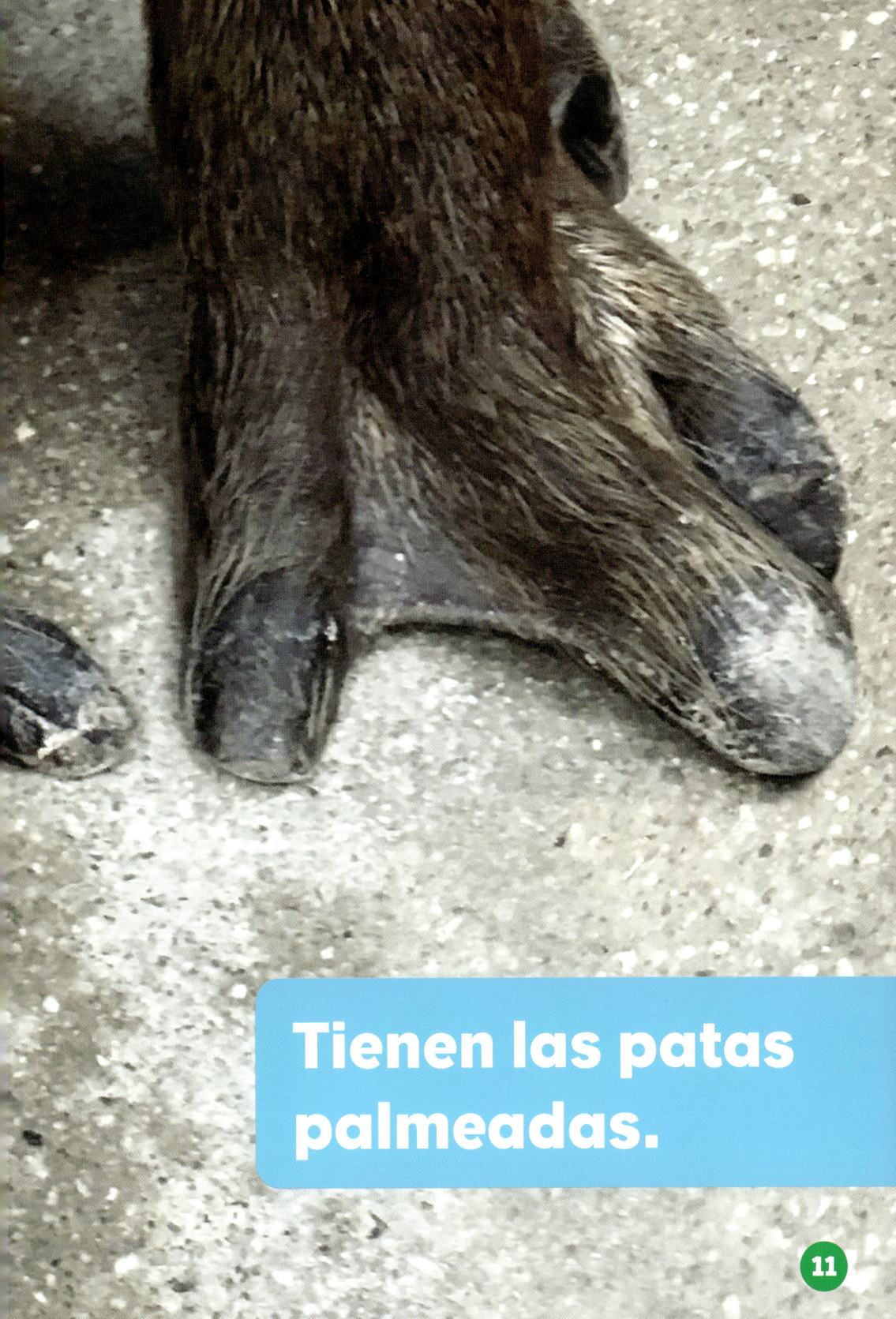

Tienen las patas palmeadas.

¡Aprenden a nadar!

Crecen.

¡REPASEMOS!

¿Qué están haciendo estos carpinchos cachorros?

ÍNDICE

cabeza 8
cachorros 3
grupo 5
nadar 13

orejas 9
palmeadas 11
patas 11
pelo 7